Library of Congress Catalog Card Number: 61-9590
Printed in the United States of America

B C D E

LET'S FIND OUT
WHAT'S IN THE SKY

by

MARTHA and CHARLES SHAPP

Pictures by Peter Costanza

FRANKLIN WATTS, INC.
575 Lexington Avenue, New York 22

What can you see in the sky?

It depends upon the time of day you look at the sky.
The sky looks different at different times.

In the daytime, the sky is light.

At night, the sky is dark.

In the daytime, the sun shines and the sky is blue.

Some days, big clouds hide the sun.
Then the sky looks gray.

There are many things to see in the sky in the daytime.
There are birds and planes and clouds . . .

. . . and the big, round sun.

The sun seems to move across the sky.
In the morning, we see the sun in the east.

In the afternoon, we see the sun in the west.

The sun's light makes shadows.
In the morning and in the afternoon, the shadows are
very long.

At lunch time, the sun is high in the sky.
Then the shadows are very, very small.

There are clouds in the sky.

Clouds have different shapes.

It's fun to look at the clouds and see the different things they look like.

On windy days, they seem like ships sailing across the sky.

On some days, the clouds are white and fluffy.

On some days, the clouds are big and dark.

The dark clouds bring rain.

Sometimes in the winter, the dark clouds bring snow.

Sometimes, after the rain, you can see a big rainbow across the sky.

There are many things to see in the sky at night. You can see thousands of stars . . .

. . . and sometimes, the big round moon.

The shape of the moon seems different every night of the month.

Sometimes it looks like this.

Sometimes it looks like this.

Look at the moon every night for a month. At first you see a little part of the moon.

Night after night, the part you see gets bigger and bigger until . . .

. . . it is a big round moon.

Then it gets smaller and smaller until . . .

. . . you can't see it at all!

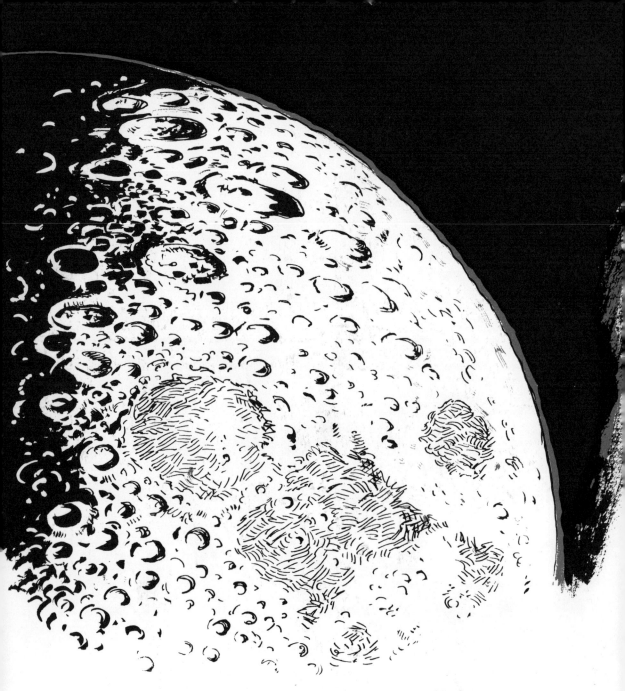

Some parts of the moon are light.

Some parts of the moon are dark.

To some people, the light and dark parts look like a
man in the moon.

There are thousands of stars in the sky.

Some stars are very bright.
Some stars are not so bright.
Some seem to twinkle.

The stars seem to make pictures in the sky.

See if you can find the Big Dipper and the Little Dipper.

There's so much to see in the sky.

VOCABULARY LIST (100 words)

a
across
after
afternoon
all
and
are
at

big
bigger
birds
blue
bright
bring

can('t)
clouds

dark
day(s)
daytime
depends
different
dipper

east
every

find
first

fluffy
for
fun

gets
gray

have
hide
high

if
in
is
it('s)

let's
light
like
little
long
look(s)
lunch

make(s)
man
many
month
moon
morning

move
much

night
not

of
on
out

part(s)
people
pictures
planes

rain
rainbow
round

sailing
see
seem(s)
shadows
shape(s)
shines
ships
sky
small(er)
snow
so

some
sometimes
stars
sun('s)

the
then
there('s)
they

things
this
thousands
time(s)
to
twinkle

until
upon

very

we
west
what('s)
white
windy
winter

you